CELTIC
SAINTS

CELTIC
SAINTS

LIVES OF THE HOLY EXILES

LAURENCE
WAREING

BIRLINN

First published in Great Britain in 2020 by
Birlinn Ltd
West Newington House
10 Newington Road
Edinburgh
EH9 1QS

www.birlinn.co.uk

ISBN: 978 1 78027 570 3

British Library Cataloguing-in-Publication Data
A catalogue record for this book is available
on request from the British Library

Designed and typeset by Mark Blackadder

Printed and bound by Bell & Bain Ltd, Glasgow

For Alex and Joel
walkers,
climbers,
seekers,
friends

Contents

Acknowledgements

Extracts from 'Mirin' by James Robertson used with permission.

I am grateful to those who have pointed me towards both saints and sources that otherwise might have eluded me, in particular Hugh Andrew, Jennifer Bell and James Robertson.

Ann Crawford and Andrew Simmons have been supportive guides along the way.

Helen, as always, has been my best critic and chief encourager.

Introduction

At low tide on An Tràigh Mhòr, 'the Big Beach' that welcomes ferries to the Isle of Tiree, sits a small, flat rock known as 'The Little Cursed One'. It is said that St Columba condemned the rock to lie forever bare after the seaweed covering it proved inadequate to the task of holding his coracle fast. Further along the same beach is a rocky outcrop whose strands of seaweed did the job more effectively; this Columba named 'The Holy Skerry'.

It is a fleeting incident that, nevertheless, sheds its own light on Columba and the other Christian leaders of Irish-Celtic heritage included in this volume. It hints at a figure with considerable authority whose sense of relationship with the natural world around him was palpable – even bearing pre-Christian echoes – and for whom the practicalities and dangers of travel were an ever-present concern.

Journeying was a core expression of Columba's faith: coracles and currachs were tangible symbols of his mission. Leaving home behind was almost a prerequisite for those we call Celtic saints: the beginning of faith commitment. In an iconic moment, the young Columbanus stepped over the prone body of his mother, who had lain down to block the doorway to their home, as he resisted her desperate attempt to prevent his departure.

While accounts of martyrdom as we usually imagine it are rare among the Celtic saints, many of these *peregrinari pro Christo* ('pilgrims for Christ') set out in witness to their faith with the clear intention of never returning to their homeland or family. Columba, himself, may have been an exception but he, like those in whose tradition he followed, placed himself, quite literally, beyond his comfort zone in ways that are almost impossible for many of us to imagine nowadays. The journeys themselves were frequently perilous: for every saint that made it across the treacherous Irish Sea (whether in a currach or miraculously perched on a leaf), one has to wonder how many drowned in the attempt.

Further, in order to establish the closest possible connection with their God, many such individuals chose to retreat to remote, hostile locations – frequently on islands or barren ocean rocks. They deliberately embraced the severely ascetic 'white martyrdom' of self-exile – a kind of living death.

Not surprisingly, their faith was closely tied to their interactions with, and respect for, the natural world through which they travelled with Bible, bell and walking staff. Though the appropriation of this form of spirituality into a modern, ecologically aware type of Christianity can be misleading, there is, nevertheless, a sense in which the pared-down lifestyles of the Celtic saints both drew upon and valued deeply a connection with God in each particular experience of the world around them.

Gott Bay, Tiree

The men and women who are representative of Celtic Christianity travelled across the territories of the Atlantic seaboard – Ireland, Wales, Cornwall – and eastward, with present-day Scotland providing fertile ground for missionary activity. Their influence is also felt strongly in present-day Northumbria. At one level, the movement was a spreading network of monasteries, with the major foundations, such as Clonard, Bangor, Iona and Lindisfarne, birthing a kind of monastic family tree that stretched into continental Europe.

The task of capturing the real human lives linked to these influential monastic foundations, and of corralling them into an orderly gathering, either by date or geography, is always going to be provisional – based, as it has to be, on the creative imagination of oral traditions.

However, by attempting a rough chronology, we can begin to build a picture of 'Celtic' Christianity emerging in the late 300s AD. At this time, the Romans were leaving Britain and Ninian, or someone like him, was establishing his missionary base in the south west of Scotland. We can see its decline from the mid-700s, by which time the Celtic strain of Christian faith was being rapidly subsumed within the form of Christianity organised from Rome. Dates are often imprecise but where something helpful can be said about them they are mentioned in the narrative.

With those parameters in mind, this necessarily representative selection of saints excludes familiar names such as Scotland's patron saint, Andrew (whose relics were a European import) and subsequent notable individuals whose lives took place outside this period, such as the highly influential Queen Margaret.

Those who have made the cut would neither have defined themselves as 'Celts' nor set themselves in opposition to the Christian tradition based in Rome. They did, however, offer a distinctive expression of Christianity characterised by what theologian James Mackey calls an 'athletic Christian spirituality'. It is unremittingly itinerant, glimpsed in countless place names, and revealed most tangibly within the physical spaces that were their holy retreats: Kildare, Clonard, Iona, Lindisfarne, Bass Rock, and even 'the big beach' on Tiree.

Abernethy Round Tower

Brigid (Bridget, Brid)
Kildare (Ireland); East Kilbride (Scotland)

Brigid emerges out of pagan religious beliefs, assuming the name of a goddess associated with fertility, healing and the divine creativity that makes life possible. As such, she embodies the early Christian tendency to transform or build upon existing religious beliefs and rites. The site of an oak tree, sacred to druidic culture, became the monastic cell or church that she established with other women at Kildare – the 'church of the oak'. An eternal fire that the women guarded, also echoing pre-Christian traditions, was surrounded by a hedge, past which no man was allowed to go. From this base, Brigid established both female and male monastic communities, calling upon Conlaed to oversee the monks. Her death, dated as the first day of February, coincided with the ancient festival of Imbolc, marking the beginning of spring. Several traditions of that day associated with Brigid, including the making of distinctive square crosses from rushes, continue to bind both Christian and pre-Christian memories together.

The complex crossover of Christian with pre-

Christian traditions and establishments embodied in the legends of Brigid is found in a number of Scottish locations where the new faith, introduced by missionaries from Ireland, built quite literally upon existing pagan and Pictish foundations. East Kilbride, for example, is a name that suggests the Gaelic for 'the clients or companions of Brigit'. Likewise, Abernethy Round Tower is one of only three Irish-style bell towers found elsewhere in the British Isles. It is associated with both an early Pictish religious foundation, with a dedication to Brigid, and a later, wealthy Christian foundation.

As a figure who transcended religious bound-aries, tradition appropriately says that Brigid was born literally in a liminal place. The illegitimate child of Bubthach, a chieftain of Leinster, and his slave Broisech, Brigid was sold while still in her mother's womb, eventually becoming the property of a druid. Fulfilling a prophesy that Brigid would be born neither indoors nor out of doors, Broisech gave birth after falling to the ground just as she had placed only one foot over the threshold of her house.

Brigid's early commitment to a life of holiness is evident from attributed miracles (as a child, she plays unharmed while surrounded by fire) and her determination not to marry. In one story, her face becomes deformed in answer to her prayers that she should not be attractive to a prospective husband (it is restored to beauty when she takes holy orders); in another, her father's attempt to marry her off to a king of Leinster is thwarted when she gives away his sword to a desperate beggar, causing the king to acknowledge her holiness.

It is the way in which Brigid's story crosses religious lines and asserts female potential that makes it so compelling. She emerges from legend as a woman both empowered and delightful. On one occasion she ran indoors and hung her cloak on a sunbeam, thinking it to be made of wood. There both cloak and sunlight remained until a sister nun pointed out her mistake. On another occasion, a king who had promised her land for a monastic foundation underestimated the young woman before him. He offered as much land as her cloak would cover. Brigid spread out her cloak, which expanded in size over many acres, forcing her condescending superior into a more realistic offer.

Ninian (Nynia)
Whithorn (Scotland)

Ninian has long been associated with Whithorn in present-day Dumfries and Galloway, and with the 'white house' (*candida casa*), a stone church he is said to have built there. But the facts surrounding his life are elusive.

The historian Bede, writing in the eighth century, describes Ninian as a Briton who evangelised amongst the 'southern Picts', so complementing the mission of Columba who worked later amongst the 'northern Picts'. However, who exactly Bede meant by the 'Picts' is debated. Indeed, this assertion, and the idea that Ninian was trained in Rome, may have been a product of Bede's own literary sources and theological leanings.

Bede's sources have Ninian arriving as early as 397 from northern England, with a sphere of authority that may have reached as far as the Isle of Man. Others argue an Irish origin: there is linguistic evidence to imply that the name Ninian may have reflected the cult of 'Finnian' of Movilla. Archaeological evidence suggests that there was no monastery at Whithorn before 500 – and one authority places Ninian as a contemporary of St Patrick and Palladius, arguing that their activities may even have overlapped. Add to this another proposal that the saint really associated with the south-west of Scotland was called Uinniau, and 'Ninian' was a figure formed by the aspirations of Northumbrian Christians such as Bede, and our grasp on any historical person called Ninian becomes considerably weakened.

An eighth-century poem, 'The Miracles of Bishop Ninian', does little to confirm the facts of the saint's life but does add colour, reflecting the lived experience of the times in which the author, and perhaps his subject, lived. One story relates how a gang of cattle reivers attempted to steal Ninian's herd of bullocks. But God 'held the thieves fast with giddiness', allowing one bull to advance with a bellowing din and kill the gang's leader – only for Ninian to restore him back to life. Another miracle tells of a crippled boy, healed and dancing in celebration after being brought to Ninian's tomb.

We are on firmer ground when talking about Whithorn itself. Here, and nearby Kirkmadrine, are homes to the oldest Christian monuments in Scotland. These include the Latinus Stone with its inscription beginning 'We praise you, the Lord', suggesting that Christianity was established in the

area by at least 450, although Ninian himself is not included in the recorded names of early Christians. The notion that *candida casa* was built by Ninian in the style of continental masons and named for St Martin of Tours (who Ninian is said to have visited on his way back from Rome) is now disputed but, by Bede's time, some such white building had established a reputation, marked by its contrast to the modest wooden structures of which there are still remains. And by the time the author of 'The Miracles' came to describe Ninian's impact on the region, he could delight in the presence of 'an excellent swarm of monks'.

Piran and Ciaran of Saighir

Perranporth, Cornwall (England); Saighir (Ireland)

Much of Piran's biography is a stolen one. An early Latin *vita* ('life') of the saint bears a very close resemblance to a life of Ciaran of Saighir, a mid-fifth-century Irish monk and bishop whose monastery became the burial place of the kings of Ossory.

In the transition from Ireland to Cornwall, his name appears to have morphed into the new name of Piran. His memorable journey earns a lively retelling on 5 March each year – the saint's day in Cornwall that he shares with Ciaran in Ireland. It describes how Piran/Ciaran angered a king in the west of Ireland and was hurled off a cliff with a mill-stone around him. Miraculously, he was able to float across what is sometimes referred to as the Celtic Sea, coming to land near the mouth of the River Camel in Cornwall.

Added to this is a tale that links the saint with the foundation of Cornwall's tin industry. As he arrives on shore, Piran is welcomed by a group of men who light a fire, perhaps to help dry out the refugee. As the heat grows more intense, white liquid starts to flow from a nearby outcrop of black rock. Piran identifies from this the possibility of smelting, which will enable the extraction of tin from its ore. Though this process in fact dates as far back as the Bronze Age, the story offers one explanation for the white cross on black that forms the design of the Cornish flag – the *Baner Peran*.

Though Piran's name is present in countless Cornish place names, few churches or chapels have commemorated him, aside from the chapel in the dunes in the parish of Perranzabuloe. Here, on what is the presumed site of Piran's oratory near Perranporth, a procession takes place annually in his honour.

Meanwhile, back in Ireland, stories have accrued around the life Ciaran, often suggesting his command over the natural world. He lived as a hermit but founded at Saighir the great monastery of Ossory. He also established a nunnery for his mother, Liadania, and her companions. Legend suggests that he pre-dated Patrick and, therefore, has claim to being the 'first-born of the saints of Ireland'. And so, as Ciaran, he remains respected in one country while, as Piran, he reflects the powerful oral imagination of another.

Patrick

Ireland

Patrick is one of the few Celtic saints whose voice we can hear from his own writings – the auto-biographical *Confessio* and an angry *Letter to the soldiers of Coroticus*. This was written to followers of a British warlord who invaded Ireland and killed or abducted a great many Christians whom Patrick had recently baptised. The letter vividly expresses the depth of Patrick's pain that the 'sheep around me are mangled and preyed upon' but it is also revealing of his attitude to the Irish people and his mission towards them:

> I live as an alien among non-Roman peoples, an exile on account of the love of God . . . Is it just from myself that comes the holy mercy in how I act towards that people who at one time took me captive and slaughtered the men and women servants in my father's home?

Patrick, like St Paul, whose voice he often seems to echo, was born a Roman citizen – his birthplace variously placed in locations as far apart as Cornwall and Kilpatrick (meaning 'Patrick's Church') on the River Clyde. His father was an estate owner and a Christian deacon, and his grandfather a priest, although Patrick himself had little interest in religion. As a teenager, he was taken into slavery by Irish raiders and worked as a sheep and pig herder for six years, during which time he turned to God and became devout. Eventually, making an arduous and miraculous escape back home, he was later ordained a deacon and subsequently a priest.

Patrick records a dream in which a messenger arrives from Ireland 'with so many letters they could not be counted'. The first one he reads contained 'the voice of the Irish people', begging him, a 'holy youth . . . to come and walk again among us'. In fact, it seems that, while absent abroad, he was appointed as a missionary bishop by British Christians and sent back to Ireland in that capacity.

His mission, usually dated from 432, was a commitment he lived out until his death. He wrote of his desire to return home and to visit fellow Christians on the continent but personal feelings were subjugated beneath passionate conviction. 'God knows what I would dearly like to do. But I am bound in the Spirit, who assures me that if I were to do this, I would be held guilty.'

Patrick had his critics. The *Confessio* alludes to personal attacks levelled at his incomplete education, his 'slowness of speech', and some unspecified youthful indiscretion. Still, though Patrick did not bring Christianity to the island (he was most likely preceded if not by Ciaran of Saighir then by Palladius, commissioned by Pope Celestine), he came to be regarded, like St Paul, as a formative pioneer of the faith, and credited himself with thousands of converts.

Famously, it is said that Patrick lit a fire on the hill of Slane in County Meath to mark the dawn of

Easter, pre-empting a druidic rite on nearby Tara and so contravening a ruling by the high king, Lóegaire mac Néill. In this way, Patrick engineered a confrontation with the king, out of which he secured the right to continue his missionary work. Whether true or not, the story symbolises the opposition Patrick faced as he sought to spread a young religion among frequently unreceptive people.

Patrick lived continually on the edges of society, expecting opposition and likely death, but responding with legendary defiance. He was single-minded, cannily bribing tribal leaders to let him travel in their regions while at the same time persuading their womenfolk to convert to Christianity, and adopting their sons as companions and students. Credited with banishing snakes from Ireland, Patrick's work was, in fact, to banish perceived evil by overcoming the dominant pagan cults of the time.

David (Dewi)

Mynyw – St Davids (Wales)

In the life of David (Dewi Sant), recorded by Rhigy-
farch around 500 years after the saint's death, three
of his defining characteristics are illustrated within
a single legend. His birth, it is said, was foretold to
his father, Sanctus, King of Ceredigion. An angel
revealed to him that, when he went hunting the
next day, he would discover three gifts: the stag that
he would pursue, a fish, and a hive of bees.

These gifts would foreshadow David's life. The
honeycomb would represent wisdom – as honey
lies embedded in wax, so David would draw out
spiritual meaning from literal utterances. The fish,
which appears to survive only on water, would
represent David's plain diet and abstinence from
alcohol. And the stag would signify power over evil,
'the ancient serpent'.

Sanctus' role in David's birth is double-edged,
the boy being conceived after Sanctus raped David's
mother, Non. Born in Mynyw, later renamed after
him, David was educated under the sixth-century
saint Illtyd and, for ten years, Pope Gregory's
missionary, Paulinus. Following a period of further

prayer and study in the Vale of Ewyas within the Black Mountains, he returned to his birthplace to found a monastery. The focus of his life was the training of his disciples and establishment of other monastic foundations, mainly in Wales but also in England's West Country and the East Midlands.

Stories of David's fifth-century mission, like those of Patrick, Kessog and others, are of a time when those who adhered to older traditions felt under threat from Christian evangelisation. The 'evil' mentioned in his birth legend, for example, surfaces in the reported attempts of a local chieftain, Baia, and his wife to rid Mynyw of David's new community. However, Baia, setting out to attack the monks, finds himself powerless to do so; instead, his cattle are unaccountably destroyed. Next, his wife sends her maids to cavort outside the monks' dwellings: a disconcerting sight for some of the men, but David persuades them that the life of faith demands resistance to temptation. It is Baia's family that is ruined, while the monastic community thrives.

Rhigyfarch also outlines the strict discipline that David demanded, reminiscent of the ancient desert monks. He describes a routine of labour in the fields (for 'carefree rest was the source and mother of vices'), balanced by regular prayer and a simple diet of bread and salted herbs. David, himself, is said to have been nourished only by river water and meadow-leek, abstaining from all animal products. The commitment of prospective community members was tested by making them stand outside the monastery doors for ten days before admittance.

This was David's preferred life – but theological controversy drew him into a wider role. He was persuaded to attend the Synod of Brefi in 519 and is said to have spoken eloquently from a hill that rose up under his feet. This enabled his voice to be clearly heard, and his convictions to overcome those who were following the teachings of Pelagius. (Pelagius, arguably the only notable theologian of the Celtic Church, had overemphasised the ability of human beings to earn their own salvation by combating sinful behaviour without sufficient reliance on the strength and forgiveness of God, thus undervaluing God's grace.)

A number of miracles are associated with David, often to do with the restoration of a person's sight, and once overcoming an attempted poisoning by his own deacon. However, it is his Christian example that evidently impressed those who, like Rhigy-farch, wished to assert his authenticity as a saint. They attributed his consecration as archbishop to the patriarch in Jerusalem, and hailed David as 'a doctrine to his hearers, a guide to the religious, a light to the poor, a support to the orphans'.

Petroc and Samson

Padstow and Bodmin (England); Dol, Brittany (France)

The lives of Samson and Petroc in the sixth century intersect on the north coast of Cornwall, though both were later identified as natives of Wales – Samson, like David, having studied from an early age under Illtyd at present-day Llantwit Major in Glamorgan.

On the death of his royal father, Petroc rejected his inheritance in favour of a monastic life, and was joined in this by sixty of his noblemen. Together, they resolved to travel 'to the shores of western Britain'. On arrival, Petroc encountered Samson, living as a hermit – a story probably derived from the existence of a later chapel dedicated to Samson near the mouth of the River Camel.

Despite lending his name to Petroc's Stow, now Padstow, Petroc was only a passing visitor. His biography has him travelling to Jerusalem and, from there, across an eastern ocean to reside on an island for seven years, 'nourished only by a single fish placed before him from time to time'. He returns to Cornwall and, with the aid of Samson and Wethnoc, banishes a dangerous serpent from the region, before committing again to a solitary religious life, perhaps on Bodmin Moor. He is often imaged in the company of a stag – which legend says he rescued from a local huntsman who subsequently converted to Christianity.

Samson, too, seems only have to passed through the region, in his case never to return. His early story speaks of jealousy on the part of fellow students, and of his departure to a monastery on Caldey Island off the coast at Tenby. This was followed by periods living as a hermit by the River Severn and visiting Ireland. In Cornwall, he is associated with St Kew, where existing monks refused to receive him. His disciples may have included Austell, Mewan and Winnoc, all of whose names appear on the Cornish map but who exemplify the desire that is characteristic of Celtic saints to deprive themselves of a settled lifestyle and to live on the margins of society, dependent solely on God's mercy.

Samson did eventually settle – but in Brittany, where his mentor, Illtyd, had also journeyed with food and aid in a time of famine. The district of Dol became Samson's base for further evangelical travels, including to Guernsey. There is some evidence to suggest that he rose to become a bishop, in which capacity he was signatory to acts of an episcopal council held in Paris in 557.

Kessog
Luss, Loch Lomond (Scotland)

Kessog is portrayed as one of the first Christian martyrs in Scotland, an inspiration to Robert the Bruce and a notable missionary. Today, he has an oil field and a modern bridge (Kessock) named after him. However, Kessog's role in the advance of Celtic Christianity has been eclipsed by Ninian, Columba, Kentigern, and even Scotland's adopted son, Andrew. It wasn't always so.

Kessog has special associations with Luss, on the west bank of Loch Lomond – and, more particularly, the island of Inchtavannach ('Monk's Isle'), where he established a monastery around 510. It was here, on a strategic waterway, that Kessog had been sent to further the missionary work of his mentor, Machaloi (perhaps 'Mo Chaoi' of Nendrum monastery in County Down), pre-dating Columba's mission by several decades.

Kessog (also referred to as Mackessog) was born in Ireland, in Cashel, County Tipperary, into the royal family of Munster. This was St Patrick's centre of mission and it is not inconceivable that Kessog studied with him. Certainly, Kessog is closely associated with the eastward trajectory of Celtic mission, with suggestions that he travelled as far north as Kessock on the Black Isle – though this may have been a later naming in his honour. Working from Luss, in an area where the kingdoms of Dal Riata and North Britain met, and identified also as a Pictish saint, his prior claim as Scotland's patron saint has merit.

To these hints of Kessog's career we may add a tale of precocious holiness. As a boy, it is said that

Inchtavannach, Loch Lomond

he was playing with the sons of visiting royalty when, in an unexplained accident, all but Kessog were drowned. Anger at the event threatened to erupt into warfare between the royal houses. However, following a night in prayer, Kessog was able to restore the visiting princes to life.

Legend has it that Kessog's own death was at the hands of mercenaries, at Bandry on the shore of Loch Lomond, overlooking Inchtavannach. Why, we don't know – though it is not hard to imagine violent religious tensions arising from the disruptive innovations of pioneering evangelists. From a Christian perspective, the task would always be an uphill struggle. In a life of St Voloc (Walloch), recorded in the sixteenth-century *Aberdeen Breviary*, the race that he set out to convert is described dismissively as 'fierce, untamed, void of decency of manners and virtue, and incapable of easily listening to the word of truth, and their conversation was rather that of brutes that perish than of men'.

The lasting impact of Kessog's work is evident in the number of churches across Scotland dedicated to his name, and the widely held belief that, at the battle of Bannockburn, some eight centuries later, Robert the Bruce inspired his soldiers by summoning the saint's memory – an honour Kessog shares with Fillan.

Teneu (Enoch, Thenew)

Traprain Law, East Lothian; Culross, Fife (Scotland)

Teneu is a hidden saint – a woman whose very name has been lost to us. If she is remembered at all, it is by virtue of a shopping centre in the centre of Glasgow: St Enoch's. Enoch is a corrupted (and more masculine-sounding) form of her name. Just nearby, however, once stood a chapel dedicated to Teneu – itself marking the site of a sacred well and ancient tree, said to be a place of healing.

Water runs through her story and that of her son – the more familiar Kentigern, or Mungo, who nowadays has a great cathedral to his name. Nothing is verifiable about Teneu's story. Possibly, she was a sixth-century Britonnic princess of the ancient kingdom of Gododdin, which includes modern-day Lothian. She is presented as the daughter of King Lleudden (or Lot) and as a devotee of the Virgin Mary, to whom she prayed that that she might imitate her in conceiving a child.

Teneu's actual experience of early motherhood was brutal. One account of her life records that she was raped by an unsuccessful suitor, the Welsh prince Owain ab Urien, who confused Teneu by disguising himself as a woman. Perhaps for this reason, in a later account, Teneu appears unsure of how she became pregnant and does not mention Owain's assault. Her father, presumably now regarding Teneu as soiled property, had her thrown from the top of Traprain Law, site of an ancient hill fort in East Lothian. Miraculously, she and her unborn child survived the fall. She was placed in a coracle to float west down the Firth of Forth, coming to rest at Culross in Fife. Here, in the safe care of the community of St Serf, she gave birth to Kentigern.

While Owain ab Urien, a historical figure, went on to become the stuff of legend in the Welsh stories of King Arthur, Teneu's life in Scotland disappears from view – though some accounts have her marrying another Welsh prince and bearing further sons. She may have been buried near the site of the well dedicated to 'St Tanew', near present-day St Enoch's Square in Glasgow. Those looking for cures from illness were known to come to the well and to make votive offerings of pieces of tin, shaped to represent the part of the body in need of healing.

Kentigern (Mungo) and Conval
Glasgow and Inchinnan (Scotland)

Kentigern's story begins with the forced exile of his pregnant mother Teneu and her rescue by Serf at Culross on the north shore of the River Forth. He named her illegitimate son 'Kentiern' ('chief' and 'lord') but, out of fondness, nicknamed him 'Mungo' ('well loved').

Kentigern, it is said, grew up as one of Serf's pupils, though a twelfth-century life of Serf makes no mention of the boy. Indeed, as the scholar John Reuben Davies argues, the mythology that surrounds Kentigern was most likely crafted some 500 years after his death in order to back up the establishment of an episcopacy in Glasgow, and the stories most closely associated with him are as much about the city as the saint.

One story describes Kentigern's departure from Culross, re-establishing himself in a cave beside the Molendinar Burn, a tributary of the River Clyde now in modern-day Glasgow. He leaves Culross on account of the jealousy of Serf's other pupils. When, for example, they kill Serf's tame robin, they push the blame on to Kentigern, who responds by

Glasgow Cathedral

restoring the bird to life through prayer.

Glasgow novelist Archie Hind imagines Kentigern's new mission beside the Clyde's shallows as 'like any inn or hostelry at the most likely place to catch the customers or converts, at the spot where the drovers or travellers would pause before crossing the ford'. His self-imposed austerity in this place exemplifies the stringent lifestyle of his calling – a stone for a pillow, the recitation of the psalms while standing in the cold river, and a dress of goatskin worn under his linen alb.

Kentigern's most prominent biographer, Jocelin of Furness, links him with the kings of Strathclyde and the northern territories, reflecting geographical terms and a distribution of power existing much later than the sixth century when he is said to have lived. Jocelin says that when Reydderch ap Tudwal (king of Clyde Rock) was usurped by Morken Mawr, Kentigern was also exiled – perhaps into Cumbria; maybe, though more doubtfully, into North Wales, where he is said to have been granted lands for the building of a monastery at Llan-Elwyn. Llan-Elwyn was subsequently renamed for one of Kentigern's pupils, Asaph, who wrote yet another early life of his former master.

The rehabilitation of Reydderach meant also the recall of Kentigern, and renewed missionary activity that reached into areas under the influence of his contemporary, Columba. The two men seem to have had a respectful friendship and are said to have exchanged pastoral staffs.

As an embodiment of Glasgow's rise to prominence, Kentigern is celebrated both in its cathedral (St Mungo's) and the city's coat of arms, which pictures a number of events in Kentigern's life, including his compassion for the wife of Reydderach. She had embarked on an affair, rashly gifting her lover a ring first received from her husband. On discovering the ring on the man's finger, Reydderach flings it into the Clyde, and confronts his wife with its loss. She appeals to Kentigern who, remarkably, retrieves the ring from the mouth of a salmon. The queen's life is spared and her lifelong penance is guaranteed.

A tradition grew up that one of those who continued Kentigern's mission was Conval, later named as one of his disciples. He had journeyed miraculously from Ireland on a large stone, dubbed 'St Conval's Chariot'. This is to be seen alongside the Argyll Stone in Inchinnan, close to Renfrew on the River Clyde, where Conval came to shore. His foundation here beside White Cart Water was the centre of his evangelistic work in present-day East Renfrewshire and, reputedly, his final resting place.

Finnian of Clonard

Clonard (Ireland); Anglesey (Wales)

Finnian's reputation is bound up with the great monastic venture that became one of the defining features of Celtic Christianity. His monastery at Clonard in Ireland would be a dominant force in the training of future monastic pioneers; and his guide to private penance – a 'penitential' – was a significant model for that of Columbanus, who in turn would spread the influence of Irish-Celtic monasticism into Europe.

At the age of thirty, Finnian, a native of Leinster, travelled to Wales. Whether he met the saints David, Gildas and Cadoc there depends on one's interpretation of a less-than-clear chronology but Finnian does seem to have absorbed the strict asceticism associated with David at Mynyw. This, in turn, would influence both the way of life at Clonard and his penitential. Finnian's weekday diet of bread, herbs and water, for example, is reminiscent of David's, though Finnian is said to have made an exception on Sundays and holy days, when he enjoyed broiled salmon and a cup of clear mead or ale. In common with other saints, he is said to have slept on bare ground with only a stone for a pillow.

Finnian returned to Ireland, evidently accompanied by British followers, and possibly via Anglesey, where the central island town of Llanffinan still bears his name. He settled for some years in Aghowle in County Wicklow, on land granted him by Muredach, the king of Leinster, and founded a further monastery in County Carlow. Then, in 530, Finnian embarked on his great enterprise – the monastery at Clonard, where he stayed until his

death in 550, possibly a victim of the plague.

Daphne Mould, a biographer of Celtic Saints, describes the level country around Clonard, with its ability to accommodate large numbers of students at any one time (3,000 estimated in Finnian's lifetime). 'It is easy to visualise', she writes, 'the scattered, hutted, settlement on the plain' and to picture Ciaran of Clonmacnoise arriving with his cow, as perhaps many students did, for provision of milk.

Ciaran is one of the 'Twelve Apostles of Ireland', who are all said to have studied at Clonard – the others including Brendan the Navigator, Cainnech and Columba. Some of them most likely pre-date Finnian but, as Mould suggests, 'what the list stands for is the formative influence that Clonard had on Irish monasticism', contributing in a major way to the movement's expansion overseas.

Ciaran of Clonmacnoise

Clonmacnoise (Ireland)

It is said that the other saints of Ireland were so jealous of Ciaran of Clonmacnoise that they prayed for his early death. Whether true or not, he was indeed still a young man when he died in the 540s, aged just thirty-three. By this time, he had founded the monastery at Clonmacnoise in County Meath, which would become one of the most important seats of learning in Ireland. It survived until the mid-sixteenth century. Ciaran is also known as 'the younger' to distinguish him from Ciaran of Saighir.

The wide influence of Ciaran and of his ascetic monastic rule would fulfil the prophesy contained in another story about him. While a student under Finnian at Clonard, Ciaran gave away his copy of the Gospel of Matthew, having studied only half of it. As a result, his peers dubbed him 'Ciaran Half-Matthew'. Finnian, though, said that a more appropriate nickname would be 'Ciaran Half-Ireland', for Ciaran would come to dominate half the island, leaving the rest for everyone else.

Stories of animals are associated with Ciaran, as with many other Celtic saints. As a boy, he incurred the wrath of his mother by feeding a newborn calf to a hungry wolf, only to restore it to life from its remains. While a student, a tame fox would carry Ciaran's written work to his master, until the fox became old enough to eat his homework. And his own cow, brought from home, was famed for the amount of milk it produced. After its death, legend has it that the monks of Clonmacnoise used its hide to create the book 'of the dun cow', an encyclopaedic collection of devotional and secular writings and the oldest Irish manuscript still in existence.

Following studies with Abbot St Enda on the Aran Islands, Ciaran travelled on the mainland of Ireland before arriving, with around ten others, at Clonmacnoise ('Meadow of the sons of Nois'). The son of a travelling craftsman and woodworker, Ciaran oversaw the building of the foundation's initial wooden structures and was the monastery's first abbot – but he died within the year.

Unlike other monastic foundations, and possibly reflecting Ciaran's lack of family connections, the position of abbot was not hereditary. The saint's personal humility is also suggested by his request that, after death, his body be left on a hillside like an animal's – a sign that his spirit was more important than any relics from his remains.

Columba (Collum Cille)
Iona (Scotland)

So closely is Columba associated with the monastery that he founded on Iona, and with the impact of that small island community on large swathes of present-day Scotland and northern England, that we may easily lose sight of other important elements of his story. Before travelling to Scotland, his influence in Ireland was such that he is regarded there as a patron saint. He lived less than half his life on Iona and, for the first half, was as much a man of war as of prayer. He was a politician as well as a priest, a copier and illustrator of the gospels as much as a visionary. We should also note that the most influential account of his life was written by a relative, Adamnán, who had a vested interest in extolling the goodness of Columba and the significance of the monastic community of which he himself became abbot in 679.

Born in 521, Columba was a member of the powerful Néill clan in Ireland and he studied under Finnian at Movilla and then at Clonard. He went on to found monastic communities in Ireland but, in 563, he was exiled in circumstances that are unclear.

One theory is that he copied out an important psalter belonging to Finnian – an early and serious breach of copyright. It certainly appears that he was involved in religious controversy and inter-clan rivalry – possibly warfare also – which was only resolved when a synod in 563 demanded Columba's departure from Ireland, possibly in return for rescinding his excommunication.

Columba was granted land on Iona by a Pictish king (possibly Conall mac Comgaill) and this became his base for the next thirty-four years. From here, he evangelised across mainland Pictish territories and established other foundations in the Inner

Iona Abbey

Hebrides – including 'Hinba', to which he would retreat for periods of solitude, and on Tiree, to which he sent penitents. He remained influential in political life, consecrating Aedan of Dal Riata in 574. Although it is said that he settled at the northern end of Iona, deliberately out of view of his homeland in order to reduce the temptation to return, in 575 he travelled home with Aedan to the Convention of Druim Cett. Here, he mediated in a dispute over the military obligations of the Irish diaspora to their overlords in Ireland.

Adamnán describes Columba as a tall figure, powerfully built. The force of his personality emerges both through the intensity of his religious discipline and in his harsh judgement on those he regarded as sinners. We read of his encounters with angels and of fighting with flying devils; and of sending an angel to save a man falling from a roof. His followers watch him at prayer through the crack in a doorway, witnessing a blinding light shining from his face; and Adamnán records his ability as a seer – predicting the approach of travellers and outcome of distant battles. The tale is even recorded of Columba encountering a great eel monster in Loch Ness and commanding it to leave well alone the monk whom he had sent swimming to retrieve a boat needed to cross over.

On Iona, Columba created discrete physical
spaces that allowed, on the one hand, for undis-
turbed monastic reflection and, on the other, for
hospitality to pilgrims, once telling a follower to
care for a visiting crane from Ireland until it became
strong and referring to the bird as a 'pilgrim' or
'guest'. Whether a voluntary exile for Christ or an
involuntary missionary to Scotland, he emerges as
a natural leader of extraordinary energy, of whose
physical and spiritual capacity Adamnán is entirely
in awe.

Cainnech (Kenneth)

Western Isles (Scotland)

Cainnech, it is said, once left his staff behind on Iona following a visit to his close friend Columba. Columba picked it up and carried it back to his oratory, where he prayed. Stopping off at Oídech (possibly the island of Islay), Cainnech lay down on the ground to pray. Looking up, he discovered his staff lying miraculously ahead of him.

It's a tale that suggests both Cainnech's occasional absentmindedness and the unique intensity of his friendship with Columba. These characteristics appear again in Adamnán's account of Columba becoming caught in a powerful sea storm, together with some companions. They beg him to pray for their safety, but Columba declares that this is not his responsibility but Cainnech's. 'In the same hour', Cainnech, just as he is breaking bread to begin a meal in his refectory back in Ireland, hears Columba's words and rushes from the room saying that 'we cannot have dinner at this time, when Columba's ship is in danger on the sea'. As he dashes to the chapel to pray, he leaves one of his sandals behind and while Cainnech's prayer summons the power to save his friend, Columba has his own vision – of Cainnech running with only one sandal on.

Cainnech and Columba probably trained together at Clonard under Finnian, and in Glasnevin on Ireland's east coast. When plague hit in 544, Cainnech escaped to Wales, returning eventually to Ireland to found a number of monasteries, most famously Aghaboe in Laois. His time in Wales may have furnished Cainnech with a knowledge of the Pictish language. This would have enabled him to act as an interpreter for Columba when they travelled together to present-day Inverness-shire to visit

Brude, in whose territories Columba was pursuing his missionary activity.

These journeys northward by Columba and his followers were the demanding requisite of their calling, but their influence was long-lasting. Drostan, another saint closely associated with Columba, is named as the founder of a monastery at Deer, in present-day Aberdeenshire. Religious communities were active here until the Scottish Reformation, playing an important role in embedding Christianity in the region.

Drostan, like so many in the Celtic tradition, ended his life as a hermit. Periods of solitariness were also important to Cainnech and are described with endearing details – his expulsion of mice from one island because they'd nibbled his shoes and his admonishment of birds for singing on the sabbath.

Cainnech's compassion, too, is recorded in an entirely believable incident in which he finds a woman freezing in the snow, with her child lying beside her. Cainnech sends companions to fetch food, and kindling for a fire. He revives the woman and restores her child.

Known as Kenneth in Scotland, his name appears especially on the west coast islands (Inchkenneth island in Loch na Keal beside Mull, Kilchennich on Tiree, Kilchaine in South Uist) and across Fife.

Donnán

Eigg (Scotland)

Donnán is unusual among Celtic saints, being known less for stories of his mission than by the manner of his death. He was murdered with his fifty or so companions, most likely on the small island of Eigg in the Inner Hebrides.

While most Celtic saints lived out the 'white martyrdom' – austere lives marked by penitence and periods of isolation – Donnán suffered 'red martyrdom', which Columba is said to have predicted when Donnán visited him on Iona to request that he become be his 'anamchara' – a soul friend, or confessor. Columba refused, saying that he would only be soul friend 'to folk of white martyrdom', whereas 'thou and the whole of thy community with thee will go to red martyrdom'.

Probably starting out in Ireland, Donnán may have travelled widely in Scotland, judging from the number of places named in his honour. They exist as far north as Caithness and Sutherland and down the west coast to Kildonan on Arran. However, he is most closely associated with Eigg, despite early sources being vague as to its actual whereabouts.

Remains of a church situated on an earlier medieval site suggest Donnán established a community in fertile land on the east coast of the island, in a place also now known as Kildonan.

Accounts of the slaughter vary. In one version, a prominent island woman takes revenge on the monks for either appropriating some of her sheep or taking over her grazing rights.* Failing to persuade other islanders to kill the men, she organises for bandits to invade the island and act on her behalf. More likely, this was the work of Vikings.

Either the monks were corralled into the refectory or, in another version, they were beheaded. The medieval Latin *Book of Leinster* offers the most detailed account:

> When [the] bandits arrived in Eigg, they found them chanting their psalms in the oratory and they could not kill them there. Donnán however said to his community: 'Let us go into the refectory so that these men

---

* In a version told in 1917 by Kenneth Macleod, a native of Eigg, it is the Queen of Moydart who takes offence at Donnán: 'I am keeping herdsmen to herd my cattle on the face of Corravine, and not to be herded themselves by a monk.' *Songs of the Hebrides* vol. 2, p. 205.

may be able to kill us there where we do our living according to the demands of the body; since as long as we remain where we have done our all to please God, we cannot die, but where we have served the body, we may pay the price of the body'. In this way, therefore, they were killed in their refectory on the eve of Easter.

The Isle of Eigg

Caten and Blane

Isle of Bute; Dunblane (Scotland)

Caten and Blane were related by blood, as well as by association with the important monastery of Kingarth on the Isle of Bute. Lasting memories of both are included in the *Aberdeen Breviary* of 1510, the first significant book to be printed in Scotland.

Least is recorded about Caten. The *Breviary* speaks of his noble Irish heritage, while a twelfth-century Irish martyrology describes him as 'Cattán the abstinent stern warrior', and 'Bláán's tutor or foster-father'. It is told that the monk Caten, a *peregrinare pro Christo* ('pilgrim for Christ'), was accompanied from Ireland to Scotland's west coast by his sister, Ertha. She subsequently gave birth to Blane illegitimately – in one account, made pregnant by the spirit of a well.

Blane was sent to Ireland for his early training. In some retellings, Ertha is banished by her brother for her infidelity and set adrift without oars until she and her newborn reach the Irish coast, where Comgall of Bangor takes them in. It is a story that finds its parallel in that of Teneu and Kentigern, although other accounts insist that Blane floated miraculously the *other* way, to commence his ministry in Scotland. Whatever the adventures of his early life, Blane appears to have been received eventually by Caten, who trained him further and made him his successor at Kingarth.

While Caten's memory is preserved largely in the Western Isles, place names suggest that Blane was more influential in central Scotland. The same martyrology speaks of 'Bláán the mild, of Mingarth and Dunblane was his chief monastery and of Kingarth is he'. He is closely associated with Dunblane, where a Christian community was established some time after Blane's death in the late 500s. As well as the ruins at Kingarth itself, remains of other chapels dedicated to Blane include those at the western end of Loch Earn, near Balquhidder.

The *Aberdeen Breviary* records several miracles associated with Blane, a number echoing biblical stories. For example, like Moses, Blane strikes a rock and causes a spring of water to appear. More distinctive is the troubling tale of when Blane, travelling back through northern England, restores to life the child of a nobleman. Blane performs the miracle three times – twice causing the child to die again because he has been revived with physical deformities. Only when the child is considered perfect does Blane consider the miracle a success.

Dunblane Cathedral

Fillan

East central Scotland

O God who didst save from death St Fillan,
Thy confessor and abbot, when he had been
thrown into the depths of a river, and didst
care for him therein for the space of a year by
angelic visitation: grant, we pray, that by the
intercession of his longed-for support we may
efficaciously be raised up.

This is the dramatic opening to the prayer for the
Feast of St Fillan as recorded in the *Breviarum Aber-
donense (Aberdeen Breviary)* of 1510. It records the
legend of Fillan's birth with 'a stone in his mouth'
– a speech impediment that earned him the nickname 'Labar', 'stammerer'. His father demanded
that Fillan be thrown into a lake or river and
drowned – but angels cared for the baby and, after
a year, he was lifted unharmed from the water by
Bishop Ibar, with whom the boy began his studies.

This Fillan, an Irish missionary associated with
St Fillans at the east end of Loch Earn, has become
confused with other Fillans, among them one who
was said to have built the first mill in Killin, and

Fillan the royal son of Kentigerna – who lived as a hermit at Inch Cailleach on Loch Lomond. The Fillan of the *Aberdeen Breviary* is very likely a composite representation of several holy men dating from the sixth to eighth centuries.

We owe the widespread strength of the cult of Fillan to King Robert I, 'Robert the Bruce'. Maybe because of support from the Abbot of Inchaffrey, who brought relics of Fillan in order to bless the Scottish troops before the Battle of Bannockburn in 1314, Robert subsequently restored the chapel dedicated to Fillan in Strathearn. This could be seen as an act of pious thanksgiving. It could also be seen as an astute political move since wherever relics of Fillan were venerated, associated gratitude to the King might also be assumed. It seems likely that Robert's patronage lies behind many of the foundations dedicated to Fillan across east central Scotland.

Brendan
Clonfert (Ireland)

The cult of Brendan grew around two accounts of the saint: of a historical figure, born *c.* 486, who founded a number of important monasteries in Ireland; and the legendary sailor who made a fabulous voyage to a land of delight – 'paradise'.

The first account is mentioned by Columba's biographer, Adamnán, and the little we know of him is laid out in a number of hagiographies. Probably born near Tralee in County Kerry, he was educated by St Ita and later by Erc, a bishop of Slane, and went on to establish monastic foundations at Ardfert, Annaghdown, Inishadroum and, most famously, Clonfert. Brendan died in *c.* 577 at the convent of his sister Briga in Enachduin and is said to have been buried facing the front door of Clonfert Cathedral.

Perhaps it was the many recorded journeys in Brendan's lifetime, to Wales, Brittany and the west coast of Scotland, that inspired his parallel reputation as Brendan the Voyager, whose Atlantic adventures were narrated in the *Navigatio Sancti Brendani Abbatis* some 300 years after his death.

The *Navigatio* follows in the Irish tradition of *immrani* – sea voyages punctuated by remarkable events. Inspired by a fellow monk, Barinthus, who has himself returned from a journey to the Isle of Delights, Brendan and fourteen fellow travellers set out on a seven-year odyssey. During its course, they encounter perils and wonders, from sea monsters and a 'paradise of birds' (fallen angels) to a benign dog that leads the sailors to a table spread with food. They even encounter – initially with great dread – Judas Iscariot, who has been permitted to cool himself from hell's scalding fires on what we may take to be an iceberg.

Some argue that the detailed, physical descriptions in the *Navigatio* are evidence of an actual journey and, in 1977, the adventurer Tim Severin tested the theory by completing a 4,500-mile Atlantic voyage in a boat built using techniques and materials only available in sixth-century Ireland.

The *Navigatio* can also be read as a multi-layered myth. It fits the pattern of the liturgical year, with each of the islands Brendan visits becoming the location for a major Christian feast. The ocean may also stand for the desert, both the setting for a penitential journey and representing the monastic life itself. As Alistair Moffatt points out, the Gaelic term for monastery, *diseart*, makes direct reference to the early Middle Eastern hermits known as the Desert Fathers.

Brendan's voyage has inspired other writers through the ages, including the poet Matthew Arnold, J.R.R. Tolkien and C.S. Lewis, whose novel *The Voyage of the Dawn Treader* bears more than a passing similarity to Brendan's own adventures.

Mirin (Mirren)

Paisley (Scotland)

'Not much is told of him', James Robertson begins, in his poem 'Mirin':

> He came from Ireland – Mirin of Benchor –
> a blink of light in the long, cold dark.
> He may have known Columba, Brendan,
>   Blane, Moluag.
> (It was an age of saints.)

To that list of possible acquaintances may also be added Comgall. If the legend is discounted that Mirin was a native of Patras in Greece and, with Relugas, was one of those who brought the bones of St Andrew to Scotland, then a more likely birthplace was in Ireland.

As a boy, Mirin is said to have been taken to Comgall's monastery in Bangor. Here, like Petroc of Wales, he renounced the inheritance of his father's wealth and instead embraced the monastic life – later becoming head of the community. Other legends, recorded in the *Aberdeen Breviary*, bear a notably close resemblance to stories of his mentor,

Comgall; for example, the restoration 'to pristine life' of a youthful brother who had fallen dead for several hours, 'burdened beyond measure by hard work and thirst'. Further tales – of a supernatural light seen in his monastic cell; of the miraculous sourcing of milk for a visiting monk – recall Columba and others. Unique to Mirin, however, may be his response to the contemptuous rejection by an Irish king, amongst whose followers he wished to preach the Christian gospel. Learning that the king's wife was heavily pregnant, Mirin inflicted the pain of childbirth on her husband who, after three days of agony, submitted to Mirin's wishes.

What serves to draw these myths, generic or otherwise, into a single life is Mirin's lasting association with the major cathedral town of Paisley, a

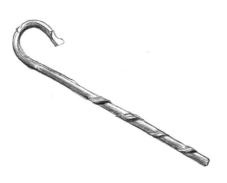

name derived most likely from the Latin for a large church, 'basilica', but more evocatively from a wood or clearing belonging to 'Paessa'. Bangor, like Iona, was an important starting place for early Christian mission, so the idea that Mirin travelled from there with evangelistic ambitions is credible. Like Conval, he based himself beside White Cart Water, perhaps building a chapel and so initiating a major religious centre to rival Glasgow and Govan. Mirin is one of the four saints to whom the Paisley Abbey was dedicated in the thirteenth century; and one of the reasons given for James IV's decision to declare Paisley a burgh in 1488 was 'the singular respect we have for the glorious confessor, Saint Mirin'.

His name is echoed in a number of Scottish place names, though even the most well-known – the island of Inchmurrin at the southern end of Loch Lomond – is more likely drawn from the female name, Muirenn. More certain is his celebration in the name of Paisley's local football team, St Mirren FC.

Probably James Robertson is right to conclude that the reality of a man such as Mirin is to be glimpsed in the image of a faithful traveller entering unknown territory, 'drifting, groping, reaching – with redemption out there somewhere in the cruel, uncharted world'.

Columbanus

Bobbio (northern Italy)

Columbanus' life begins with a flight from temptation. We are told of a young man faced with the
ordinary desires of adolescence and the temptation
to pursue a comfortable life, but whose response is
less than ordinary. He seeks advice from a local
woman, a hermit, who tells him that his desires
cannot be overcome except by leaving his home.
His distraught mother lies across the threshold of
their house in a desperate bid to prevent her son's
departure – but Columbanus steps over her and
begins a life that exemplifies voluntary exile for
Christ.

Columbanus spent time training as a monk at
Comgall's monastery in Bangor, known for its strict
discipline, until he departed for Gaul in *c.* 590. Over
the next twenty-five years, he travelled in Europe,
founding monastic houses in present-day France,
Austria and Italy. For the first of these, Annegray in
the foothills of the Vosges mountains, he appears to
have been granted use of deserted Roman buildings.
The last of his foundations, in Bobbio, became
famous for the richness of its library.

Though Columbanus was known for his oneness with nature – pre-figuring St Francis in the way small animals were drawn to his gentleness – his more widespread legacy was an austere rule, with an emphasis on physical mortification. This set his foundations apart from others on the continent. 'The extent of your prayer should be until tears come,' he wrote. 'The measure of your work should be to labour until tears of exhaustion come.' Perceived vice was punished with beating, and monks ill with flu were made to go and thresh wheat until the physical work opened their pores and expelled the fever. Neverending weariness was as much a part of Columbanus's monastic ideal as unceasing prayer.

It was a way of life Columbanus was forced to defend, even enduring an abortive attempt to repatriate him to Ireland. He insisted on the loyalty of his communities to the Pope in Rome but declared that papal authority derived not from protocol or succession but from the exercise of divinely given principles. His own penitential practice brings into sharp focus our understanding of Celtic mission and commitment. He described human existence as 'the wayfaring of mortals and not their living'. It is 'the way that leads to life but not life itself'. We are, Columbanus said, *hospes mundi*, guests of the world.

Aidan

Lindisfarne (England)

'Had it not been for the defeat and death of Edwin, the first Northumbrian Christian king,' observes historian E. Sprott Towill, 'Aidan would probably have lived and died a simple monk in the monastery of Iona'.

In 616 Edwin, not yet a Christian, had defeated Aethelfrith, King of Bernicia, causing Aethelfrith's children – Oswald, Oswin and their sister, Ebba – to flee into exile among the Gaelic-speaking Scots. They arrived on Iona, where the young royals were converted to Christianity. Meanwhile, Edwin converted to the Romanised form of Christianity brought north by the missionary, Paulinus. After Edwin himself was killed by the Welsh king, Cadwallon, Oswald returned to reclaim his homeland. Here, inspired by a vision of Columba, he defeated Cadwallon at Deniseburna near Hefenfelth ('Heavenfield') in Northumbria.

Oswald now requested a bishop from Iona who would help him re-establish Christianity in Northumbria – this time in its Irish-Celtic form. First, he was sent Corman, who found Oswald's people to be 'intractable, obstinate and uncivilised'. Back on Iona, Aidan stepped forward to suggest that perhaps they simply required a more nurturing approach. As a result, he was consecrated bishop and sent to establish a monastic centre on Lindisfarne, 'Holy Island', off the Northumbrian coast. He remained here until his death in 651. Oswald himself acted on occasions as Aidan's translator.

There are miracles associated with Aidan – including his powerful prayer that drove fire away from the gates of Bamburgh Castle, which was under attack from the Mercian army. However, it

Lindisfarne Causeway

was Aidan's example of abstinence and care of others that marked him out as an influential religious leader.

On one occasion, following the death of Oswald – the region having now divided under the authority of two kings, Oswiu and Oswine – Oswine gifted Aidan a horse to aid his travels, despite the fact that he was known to travel only on foot. Later, Aidan met a beggar on the road and offered him the horse 'with all its royal trappings to the beggar; for he was extremely compassionate, a friend of the poor and a real father to the wretched'. Aidan habitually used gifts of money to redeem slaves, many of whom he then brought to work and train in his monastery, offering them education and opportunity.

Bede notes that Aidan was respected even by those of the Roman Christian persuasion who did not always share his views, and concludes that 'the best recommendation of his teaching to all was that he taught no other way of life than that which he himself practised'.

Ebba (Aebbe)
Coldingham (Scotland)

Memories of Ebba, abbess of Coldingham in the Scottish Borders, reflect a period recorded by Bede when the influence of Irish-Celtic Christianity was being absorbed within the dominant Roman form of the faith. The two traditions disagreed about the dating of Easter and the style of monks' tonsures, issues that would be argued out at the Synod of Whitby hosted by Hilda in 664 and resolved in favour of the Roman Church.

The shift was reflected north of the border, for example, in the life of Curetán. His possible adoption of the Latin name Boniface, and a complicated hagiography that has him arriving on the Black Isle in Moray from Palestine via Rome, supports the idea that he was one of those who helped draw the Celtic and Roman traditions closer together. He is named as a signatory to the *Cáin Admonáin* (Law of Adamnán), agreed in 697 and guaranteeing protection to women and non-combatants in times of war.

As a young princess of Bernicia (encompassing present-day Northumbria), Ebba's own upbringing was shaped by civil war. She was sent for her safety into exile on Iona where, as Bede puts it, she and her brothers, Oswald and Oswiu, were 'taught in the faith as the Irish taught it and . . . regenerated by the grace of baptism'.

Eventually returning with her brothers to their home territories, Ebba embraced a monastic existence, first on the site of a deserted Roman fort on the banks of the River Derwent and then on the coast at Coldingham, north of Bamburgh. Here, she founded a community of monks and nuns. Traces of her foundation still exist at St Abb's Head, where men and women lived in beehive huts made from

mud and branches, protected on one side by the sea and on the other by a turf rampart.

It was a foundation that is best remembered for being burnt down. In his *Ecclesiastical History*, Bede tells us that an older monk, Adamnán, reported to Ebba a vision he had received of the monastery's impending destruction: God's punishment for the community's departure from strict prayer and devotion. Adamnán said, evidently to Ebba's surprise, that rooms built for prayer had become 'places for feasting, drinking, gossiping and frivolity' and that women were 'weaving elaborate garments . . . as if they were brides, so imperilling their virginity, or else to make friends with strange men'. Humbled, the community at first repented, so receiving a stay of execution; but after Ebba's death *c.* 683, it reverted to its earlier lifestyles, resulting in divine destruction of the foundation by fire.

Bede's account probably reflects his own prejudices, against both the influence of Celtic traditions and monastic foundations that housed women and men together. He excludes Ebba herself from condemnation (though barely); nevertheless, one senses that the austere self-discipline and ideals of vocation represented by Adamnán and Ebba's peripatetic forebears had here wilted within the more settled comforts of community living.

Bega (Bees)
St Bees Head, Cumbria (England)

One saint or two? A reclusive anchoress in Cumbria or the head of the first nunnery in Northumbria? With Bega, or 'Bees', as priest and scholar Sabine Baring-Gould acknowledged, 'the confusion, which is so general in the debatable ground between legend and history, becomes nearly inextricable'.

The core of Bega's story is this. Born into Irish royalty, this young woman of great beauty committed herself to a holy life. As a sign of this, an angel gave her a bracelet, which would become a holy relic following her death. Finding herself promised to a prince of Norway, Bega fled Ireland and was carried across the Irish Sea to the west coast of Scotland, variously on a cutting of turf or a leaf. Here, on the headland now known as St Bees Head in Cumbria, her story diverges into two accounts.

In one telling, she approaches Lord Egremont and requests land on which to build a priory. Cynically – it being midsummer – the nobleman offers her as much land as is covered by snow the next day. Miraculously, the following morning the entire area between his castle and the sea is white with snow, and so Bega founds her settlement.

To modern ears, Bega's implied qualities of leadership are perhaps diluted by subsequent memories of her carrying out domestic chores for the men who built her monastery. However, she was also remembered as an advocate for the poor and oppressed – including, in the Middle Ages, by those who endured raids by the Scottish Border reivers.

In another telling, Bega lived as a hermit and was fed by wild birds but, following harassment by invaders to the area, she followed the counsel of King Oswald of Northumbria to enter a priory and was received into holy orders by Aidan. She later became associated with Copeland Priory, near Carlisle, as well as St Bees itself.

One possibility is that the dangers of living a solitary life forced Bega east, towards Oswald and Aidan's territories. However, Bega's story has become entangled with those of two other religious women – Heiu and Begu – active in Northumbria, whose own histories have also become intertwined. Bede writes of Heiu of Hartlepool, inspired by Aidan and founder of a nunnery, the leadership of which she subsequently passed over to Hilda. He also writes of Begu, remembered for her vision of the death of Hilda from her own nunnery in Hackness.

Cuthbert

Lindisfarne (England)

The life of Cuthbert, perhaps more than any other, illustrates the tension that many Celtic saints felt between the imperatives of mission and meditation – between the task of convincing ordinary people that eternal salvation was an urgent necessity and the monastic calling to prayer and reflection.

Brought up within a higher-class, Anglo-Saxon family and probably with experience on the battle-field, a vision of Aidan being carried towards heaven convinced Cuthbert to turn to the monastic life. He was trained with the guidance of Boisil at the monastery in Melrose, a daughter house of Aidan's community on Lindisfarne. Called himself to be prior of Lindisfarne at some point following the great Synod of Whitby in 664, Cuthbert engaged fully in the work of his community, as missionary and healer. However, his instinct was for an austere form of monasticism and he developed a discipline of contemplative retreats on an islet adjoining Lind-isfarne, eventually committing himself to the life of a hermit on the more remote island of Inner Farne.

Cuthbert's reclusive life would have been a harsh

one: foraging for the eggs and flesh of sea birds to feed on, riding out storms, mending damaged shelters. To this, add his already ascetic lifestyle. Bede describes otters sweetly drying the saint's feet with their fur and warm breath, but this was a postscript to a night-time vigil spent in the cold sea with waves swelling up to Cuthbert's neck as his chants were swept away on the wind.

Such actions were part of Cuthbert's overriding purpose: to counter the power of evil forces, felt to be a very present reality in the world around him. One tale describes demons attacking a village with fire while Cuthbert was preaching nearby. Attempts by villagers to quench the fires with water were futile, and yet Cuthbert's demand that the fires be extinguished put the spirits to flight. The task of defending people's souls, as described in Cuthbert's story, is a tangible one.

Towards the end of his life, Cuthbert reluctantly accepted election to the bishopric of Hexham and, subsequently, Lindisfarne. However, he returned to Inner Farne to die and was buried in 687 on Lindisfarne. Here, eleven years later, it was revealed that the saint's body had not decomposed.

The brutal raids by Vikings in the 800s caused the monks of Lindisfarne to abandon the island, and Cuthbert's body was taken with them, only given a final resting place over a hundred years later in Durham.

Maelrubha

Applecross (Scotland)

Next to Columba, wrote William Reeves in 1861, 'there is no ecclesiastic of the ancient Scottish Church whose commemorations are more numerous in the West of Scotland than St Maelrubha, or whose history is marked with greater exactitude'.

Maelrubha was born in Derry, Ireland, in 642, into the clan of Eoghan. This made him a direct descendent of Niall of the Nine Hostages who, legend has it, was responsible for abducting the teenage Patrick to Ireland. A relationship on Maelrubha's mother's side with Comgall, Abbot of Bangor in County Down, has been speculated upon but is not very likely. However, it was to Comgall's monastery that Maelrubha was sent to train and from where, aged twenty-nine, he set out for the west of Scotland in search of new bases for Christian mission. Some argue that, by that stage, Maelrubha himself had become abbot at Bangor and there is evidence that connections were maintained with Bangor by his successors.

A two-year gap exists between Maelrubha leaving Bangor and settling at Applecross in the Pictish territory of Wester Ross, where his main monastic foundation was established. The time taken to locate a suitable site – and the remoteness of his choice – suggests that the journey was one of deliberate self-exile. Despite the isolated location of Applecross, however, the community's mission seems to have spread widely – with foundations bearing his name, in some form or other, from Keith in Banffshire to Crail in Fife and Ashaig on Skye. At Ashaig, it is said that one day, as the aging Maelrubha was attempting to stand up, he grabbed hold of an ash tree. It uprooted and a spring with healing properties started to flow freely from the soil.

Healing was also associated with Isle Maol Rubha on Loch Maree, north of Applecross. Here, adjacent to an oratory, a holy well and tree attracted visitors in need of healing, particularly those afflicted by mental ill-health.

Despite William Reeves's confident claims, contradictory assertions about the nature and location of the saint's death have arisen out of confusion both with Gaelic place-names and with the name of a martyred Roman saint, Rufus. The suggestion that he was killed by Danish invaders is unlikely. His grave is said to be beneath a low mound at Applecross which, with an oval enclosure, is all that remains of Maelrubha's monastery.

Dympna (Dymphna)

Geel (Belgium)

Dympna's eligibility for inclusion in a survey of Celtic saints is debatable. She is a striking example of how a *vita* can be appropriated for diverse purposes – from the founding of a hospital for the mentally ill to the inspiration for a horrifying fairy tale. Yet there appear to be no discernible historical facts relating to her and, although tradition has it that she was the daughter of a Celtic king, there is no evidence to support the view that she came from Ireland.

Said to have existed in the seventh century, Dympna has sometimes been confused with Damnat, a nun from Tydavnet in County Monaghan, Ireland, whose crozier, like Ebba's ring, became a relic on which to swear reliable oaths. The association with Damnat is incorrect, though it lingers in the modern twinning of Tydavnet with Geel in Belgium.

Also like Ebba, Dympna's story centres on flight from an unwanted marriage; in this case an incestuous union desired by her royal father. While Dympa was still young, her mother had died, extracting a promise from her husband that he would only remarry if he met a woman as beautiful and good as she had been. Tragically, Dympna grew up to be exactly that. With her confessor, Gerebernus, she escaped, first to Antwerp and then to Geel,

with the support of the court fool and his wife who disguised the pair as *jongleurs*. Their decision to then live as solitaries in a forest near Geel symbolises the desire to live as an outcast, typical of many Celtic saints.

Dympna gave care to the poor and sick in the region. However, she was tracked down by her father after distinctive coins used during her escape were recognised by his servants. The servants killed Gerebernus but balked at the idea of murdering Dympna – an act that her father carried out himself. It is a story that feminist 'mythographer' Marina Warner suggests may have caught the imagination of Charles Perrault, the nineteenth-century creator of the darkly sinister Bluebeard.

It is the father's actions, too – excused as diabolical madness – that later led to Dympna being venerated as a healer of pilgrims with mental ill-health. When her alleged remains were uncovered in the thirteenth century, they apparently stayed miraculously rooted to the spot. A church was built there, and later a hospital. Geel itself developed a pioneering reputation for care in the community of those registered at the hospital.

Baldred

Bass Rock, East Lothian (Scotland)

Few saints of the Celtic world evoke more clearly than Baldred of Tyninghame the form of 'living death' peculiar to the most ascetic monks and hermits. These were men and women who sought isolation akin to a desert existence – on hilltops, in valleys, on islands. An extreme example was the community of monks perched in their beehive shelters on Skellig Michael, off the west coast of Ireland. In the forbidding Bass Rock, opposite the coast of East Lothian, Baldred chose an especially iconic and perilous location on which to pare down his existence to the basics of naked faith.

Baldred has often been identified as a friend and pupil of Kentigern. However, the chronicler Symeon of Durham records an eighth-century Baldred, possibly born in Ireland but eventually sent north from Lindisfarne to Tyninghame, where the monastery he founded owned large areas of the coastal plain of East Lothian. This is reflected in the cult of Baldred that grew up around four churches in the area: Auldhame, Whitekirk, Tyninghame and Prestonkirk.

Whatever the management and missionary responsibilities that must have belonged to the 'the Apostle of the Lothians', Baldred's reputation comes down to us as one who chose to step aside from the run of life to test and build his spiritual strength. Sometimes he lived in a cave in the rock-face on Seacliff Beach – known as 'St Baldred's Cave'; more strikingly, he also stayed in his small hermitage on the Bass Rock.

The Bass Rock

Two particular miracles are associated with him. Feeling compassion for sailors negotiating a treacherous reef between the rock and the mainland, Baldred caused it to move into shore. It became 'St Baldred's Boat' – an outcrop that juts into the sea north of Seacliff beach.

The second miracle, an early example of cloning, followed Baldred's death, and was recorded by the nineteenth-century writer A.I. Ritchie:

> There was a dispute between the parishes of Auldhame, Tyninghame, and Prestonkirk, as to which should have his body . . . By the advice of a holy man, they spent the night in prayer. In the morning three bodies were found, in all respects alike, each in its winding sheet, prepared for burial.

Baldred's monastery was destroyed by Danish invaders in the 900s. Miracles continued to be recorded, most particularly by those who drank from St Baldred's well, near Auldhame. His remains – the Tyninghame relics – were, like Cuthbert's, transferred to Durham.

Further reading

While additional information can be sought out for individual saints, the following resources provide helpful starting points and context.

Baring-Gould, S., *The Lives of the Saints*, (rev. 1914: Edinburgh, John Grant) – a multi-volume compilation of many of the most well-known stories about individual saints

Bede, *The Ecclesiastical History of the English People*, McClure, J. and Collins, R., eds (1969: Oxford, Oxford University Press)

Farmer, D., *Oxford Dictionary of Saints*, 5th edition (2003: Oxford, Oxford University Press) – especially for additional sources

Mackey, James P., ed., *An Introduction to Celtic Christianity* (1989: Edinburgh, T&T Clark)

Macquarrie, A., ed., *Legends of Scottish Saints: readings, hymns and prayers for the commemorations of Scottish saints in the Aberdeen Breviary* (2012: Dublin, Four Courts Press)

Moffatt, Alistair, *Scotland: A History from Earliest Times* (2015: Edinburgh, Birlinn)

Mould, D.P., *The Irish Saints* (1964: Dublin, Clonmore and Reynolds Ltd)

Sprott, Towill, E. *Saints of Scotland* (1978: Edinburgh, Saint Andrew Press)

https://saintsplaces.gla.ac.uk 'Saints in Scottish Place-Names'

Other books and articles mentioned in connection with specific saints.

Baldred A.I. Ritchie, *The Churches of Saint Baldred: Auldhame, Whitekirk, Tyninghame, Prestonkirk* (reprinted 2019: London, Forgotten Books)

Brendan *Navigatio Sancti Brendani Abbatis* trans. John O'Meara and Jonathan Wooding, in *The Voyage of Saint Brendan: Representative Versions of the Legend in English Translation*, ed. W.R.J. Barron and Glyn S. Burgess (2002: Exeter, University of Exeter Press); C.S. Lewis, *The Voyage of the Dawn Treader* (1952, reprinted 1967: Harmondsworth, Penguin Books)

Columba *Adomnan's Life of Columba* ed. A.O. Anderson (1961: London, T. Nelson)

David *Rhigyfarch's Life of David*, ed. J.W. Jones (1967: University of Wales, Board of Celtic Studies)

Donnán Marjory Kennedy Fraser and Kenneth Macleod, eds, *Songs of the Hebrides* (1909–21: London, Boosey and Co.)

Dympna Marina Warner, *From the Beast to the Blonde: on Fairy Tales and Their Tellers* (1995: London, Vintage)

Kentigern Archie Hind, *The Dear Green Place* (1966, reprinted 2008: Edinburgh, Polygon)

Maelrubha William Reeves, 'Saint Maelrubha: His History and Churches', *Proceedings of the Society of Antiquaries of Scotland*, III (1857–60)

Ninian W. Levison, 'An eighth-century poem on St Ninian' (1940: *Antiquity* XIV)

Patrick Patrick's *Confessio* and *Letter to the soldiers of Coroticus* (Royal Irish Academy, www.confessio.ie)

Index of saints

In this listing, the lives of saints re-told in full are in **bold** type. Others listed, Celtic and otherwise, have been mentioned either because of their association with the featured saints (as teachers, associates, disciples) or by comparison (e.g. St Patrick and St Paul). A quick glance down the list is just one indication of the many interconnections between these lives. Common alternative names (including Gaelic and Welsh) are given in brackets.